Homage and Courtship

Homage and Courtship

(Romantic Stirrings of a Young Man)

Shadrach A. Ambanasom

Langaa Research & Publishing CIG
Mankon, Bamenda

Publisher:
Langaa RPCIG
Langaa Research & Publishing Common Initiative Group
P.O. Box 902 Mankon
Bamenda
North West Region
Cameroon
Langaagrp@gmail.com
www.langaa-rpcig.net

Distributed outside N. America by African Books
Collective
orders@africanbookscollective.com
www.africanbookscollective.com

Distributed in N. America by Michigan State
University Press
msupress@msu.edu
www.msupress.msu.edu

ISBN: 9956-616-58-3

Revised Edition with an Epithalamion

DISCLAIMER

The names, characters, places and incidents in this book are either the product of the author's imagination or are used fictitiously. Accordingly, any resemblance to actual persons, living or dead, events, or locales is entirely one of incredible coincidence.

Contents

PART I: HOMAGE

PART II: COURTSHIP

Dedicated to my Muse

Introductory Essay

SHADRACH Ambanasom's creative pen has once more graced our literary shores with a scintillating collection of sixty-two poems crafted "essentially in a Neo-Romantic mood" and being in the main, "transmutations and commemorations of things, events, and people" the poet holds dear in his life.

The structural pattern of the collection bears witness to this defining sentence given the work's division into two distinct equal parts, titled Part 1 *Homage* (31 poems) and Part 2 *Courtship* (31 poems).

Generally, the titles of the parts delineate the broad thematic preoccupations of the collection, but besides questions of honour, tribute and courtship, the poems negotiate the childhood kingdom, the transience of life, technology, nature and nostalgia, among other concerns.

The poems in the first part pay homage to icons and beacons at the family and community levels, to places and to significant milestones in the poet's experience.

Poems like "Abendong', "Icon and Beacon", "The Talented Three", "Ebang Iroko", "The Last Salute", and "A Grain of Corn" deal with the loss of loved ones. Here, the pain of loss, man's helplessness in the face of death, the devastating consequences of death at the personal and communal level are underscored through imagery, allusions, alliterations and repetitions. In most of these poems, the natural environment integrates the poetic experience as a purveyor of mood and attitude.

In "Icon and Beacon", for example, we are told that the passing of Babila John Njingum, has left 'frightened flora and fauna unprotected' and the ENSABIAN landscape is now 'an endangered habitat at the mercy of ogres'.

In these examples, landscape metaphors serve to highlight the frailty of human life in the face of wickedness and determined evil. Furthermore, the structural repetition of it tolls accentuates the music of lament and reinforces the idea of the inevitability of death. In "Abendong", the messianic stature of Zacharias Abendong in Dudum is emphasised through references to myth and the obvious parallels between this son of the native soil and Jesus Christ. The effect of this man's demise on the community assumes apocalyptic proportions in the following lines:

Discordant sounded the music of the spheres,
the sun spun around the other planets,
graves and tombs stood gaping
when Zacharias Abendong
from the world closed his eyes and breathed his last.

The parallels between Abendong and Lucas Achamba of *Son of the Native Soil* fame will not escape the sensitive reader, especially, as the poet discloses the relationship between the writing experiences of both works in the preface to the first edition.

"One Year Old", "Alma Mater", "The Ruined Palace", "The Changed Grove", and "Ode to Sabga" celebrate events and places dear to the poet. "Alma Mater", for example, pays tribute to the poet's alma mater, CPC Bali, one of Anglophone Cameroon's famed institutions of learning, lifting it above the ordinary run of educational establishments in the country.

We are told in the poem that the college is 'the rippling pool of bottomless lore,' 'a solicitous mother hen', 'pride of our fatherland', and 'trumpeter of hope.' These metaphors are carefully selected to delineate the stature of CPC and underline the poet's attitude towards this institution.

"The Dreadful Monster", "A Plea for Mercy", "Hoarded Impressions", "4 Ways to Dispatch Yourself", and "Indifferent Nature" are philosophical musings on the HIV/ AIDS pandemic, growing old, the threat of the nuclear holocaust and the negative effect of excesses of any kind.

"4 Ways to Dispatch Yourself", in effect, is a humorous jibe at our 'beer guzzling culture' with its disastrous effects on those who want to become "famous fuddler(s)".

There are clear, or metaphorical vectors of, political issues embedded in poems like "The Mediators", "A Plea For Mercy", "The Golden Mean", "The Tallest Iroko", "The Horse Rider" and "The Mosquito."

The courtship poems are focalised on Lady Zee, the poet's Muse, who inspires him to write passionate poetry celebrating her physical and moral excellence. Lady Zee is 'sans pareil' because her beauty is natural and untainted as we find in poems like "You are the Best", "All for a Face", "Beauty beyond Compare" and "My Superstella."

We encounter the speaker's ardent passion for this woman and her effect on him in "Her Smiles", "We are One", "On Meeting Lady Zee", "A Universal Tyrant", "Breathtaking Beauty", and "If I were To Hate my Lady".

What we gather from these poems is that the lover cannot resist loving his beloved and each time passion is remembered, it is celebrated. At another level, romantic love and nature fuse together to highlight the reciprocity of love in "Go and Tell Lady Zee", "She Brightens All", "A Moment Ago", "Telepathy" and, above all, the majestic "Epithalamion" or "Ode to Lady Zee", that grand, wedding song which appropriately concludes the courtship section.

In "Go and Tell Lady Zee", for instance, the wind becomes a harbinger of love, a natural messenger who must urgently inform the mistress of the poet's feelings. In pure romantic overtones, the month of May (when nature is reborn) becomes the month of celebrating reciprocal love of the kind existing between the poet-persona and his lady. This is romantic in perspective. Repetitions of words and phrases equally signal the urgency of communicating the emotion of love and loyalty to the mistress.

Where love and passion meet, they cannot but call forth desires and wishes for the beloved. One of these aspirations is for her to "become our own Jane Austen" given her "growing interest in [his] songs" and "alert mind on the way to fictional adventure." This is the dominant idea in "The Dream" and "Future Woman of Letters." With the mention of Lady Zee in the last stanza of "Ode to Sabga Heights", we have the beautiful transition from Part One to Part Two of the work. Lady Zee therefore smoothly liaises between homage and courtship.

Ambanasom's poetic territory is wide, signalling the hybridism of the poet whose effective blending of African and European experiences achieves harmony of thought and technique in the collection. It is in this wise that we discern echoes of oral tradition in "A Wise Dwarf", 'reminiscences of the Nigerian Gabriel Okara and Wole Soyinka in "The Sky Weeps" and "On Losing my Hair", respectively.

Tennysonian, Spenserian, Shakespearean, Wordsworthian, Donnean and Blakean parallels are observable in "The Last Salute", "The Dream", "Her Smiles", "The Mosquito", "The Horse Rider", "Telepathy" and "The Caged Lion". All these influences give the poetry both an African and a global appeal in these times when our destinies are unmistakeably assuming multicultural dimensions.

The richness of a poem, C. K. Stead has told us, is heightened by the appropriate use of words to expose mood and atmosphere. In this collection, Ambanasom inserts the appropriate word for the appropriate emotion, using images to clothe his thought, images assembled from things actually seen and intimately known. In addition, the poetry achieves music and rhythm through diction, alliteration, repetition, assonance and the rhythmic cadence of the structure of some of the poems. This, to my mind, constitutes the forte of the poetry.

By Eunice Ngongkum (PhD), is Senior Lecturer, Department of African Literature, University of Yaoundé 1
(This essay, only slightly updated, was initially a review that first appeared in *The Post* No. 0992 of Monday, October 6, 2008 page 8)

Preface to the Revised Edition

The revised edition is substantially a reprint of the first with a few corrections here and there. Twelve new poems have been added, that is, three under *Homage* and nine under *Courtship*. In other words Part I now contains thirty-one poems and Part II thirty-one poems, both making a total of sixty-two poems. However, the most significant innovations are Lady Zee's reply and the consequent 'Epithalamion' ('Ode to Lady Zee'), the longest poem in the collection, and a logical conclusion to the courtship poems. Since the ultimate goal of a typical courtship is marriage, nothing could be more fitting than a grand, nuptial song to crown the romantic efforts of the poet – persona who has been wooing his beloved in a series of amoretti (little loves or cupids) for several years.

Going through the poems in this collection, students of English or African literature will surely notice the multiplicity of literary influences on me, one of them being the work of Edmund Spenser, the great English Renaissance poet, after whose 'Epithalamion' mine is only roughly modelled. Spenser himself had patterned his own epithalamion on those of the ancients, for the writing of wedding songs is an old poetic tradition. The practice has a pedigree going back to antiquity and its iconic figures like Pindar, Sappho, Theocritus (Greek), Catullus (Roman), and the relatively modern Ronsard (French).

My love for English poetry dates as far back as the late nineteen seventies when I was an external undergraduate in the University of London. At that time I was only one of the many foreign students from far-flung countries like Belize, Malaysia, the Philippines, South Korea, China, Tanzania, Kenya, Nigeria and the West Indies, etc. But the bulk of the external students came from South-East Asia and the Chinese sub-continent with those intriguing, emphatic three-syllabic names like Wao Ching Tao, Konglim Tar etc.

At the end of each year the University of London came out with an annual evaluative report on students' performances. In one report without mentioning me by name, but in an obvious gesture of positive reinforcement, it referred to my fresh response to a question on Edmund Spenser's poetry in which I had quoted part of my own sonnet inspired by the English author. That sonnet is 'Her Smiles.'

Many years later, I told myself that if, as an undergraduate, I had made an impression on the University of London Examination Board with just a fragment of a poem, then I could put together some of the other poems I had since written to see whether or not they were publishable. The rest of the story is contained in the Preface to the First Edition.

With the inclusion of the espousal ode (Epithalamion), consequent upon Lady Zee's reply, 'The Symphony,' the revised edition, as it now stands, is more complete in a way that the first was not.

Shadrach A. Ambanasom
Bambili – Bamenda, Cameroon, October 2009

Preface to the First Edition

When a writer in his fifties publishes a work with the rather curious sub-title: 'Romantic Stirrings of a Young Man,' he owes the reading public a little explanation because, except in spirit, such a man can no longer be regarded as a youth. Accordingly, it is safe to say that most of the poems in this volume belong to my youthful past, with the earliest poem, 'A Wise Dwarf,' dating as far back as 1974, the year I enrolled as an external undergraduate in the University of London to read English through the correspondence course, known now as distance education. By 1981, the year I left Cameroon for postgraduate studies in Ohio University, Athens, Ohio (U.S.A.), nearly all the poems in Part I: *Homage*, my novel, *Son of the Native Soil*, and some of the poems in Part II: *Courtship*, had been written. The remaining poems under 'Courtship' continued to be written alongside the polishing of the novel until the revised edition of the latter in October 2006.

The main character of the novel is Achamba, a young man in his early thirties who is courting the text's heroine, Echunjei. The 'courtship' poems were thus written in the spirit of the hero wooing the heroine. Ultimately, however, these poems, constructed essentially in a Neo-Romantic mood, are the transmutation and commemoration of things, events, and people I hold dear in my life.

But how the poems came to be assembled as a collection is the consequence of the commingling of a peculiar set of literary circumstances at the centre of which was Professor John N. Nkengasong, of the English Department, University of Yaoundé I and President of the Anglophone Creative Writers' Association, (ACWA). Under his dynamic impetus, many Anglophone Cameroonian creative works have been published with the help of subvention from the Ministry of

Culture. Since I had not benefitted from the largesse of the Ministry of Culture for the simple reason that I had never applied for financial assistance, Professor Nkengasong was constantly urging me to do so, and would not take 'no' for an answer.

He was never satisfied whenever I said I had no unpublished creative work to submit to the Ministry of Culture for consideration. He accorded me an unusual welcome when I was in Yaoundé recently: 'Hi Prof, before I welcome you to Yaoundé, let me remind you that you have to send something to the Ministry of Culture for possible publication.' That was in August 2006 when I went down to Yaoundé in connection with a Ph.D. defence.

Thereafter I gave his 'importunity' serious thought. Then lately, I had a sudden flash of insight; I landed on the idea of the poems of my youth and those inspired by the young man in my novel. I put them together and sent them to Professor Nkengasong, asking him to see whether or not they were worth sending to the Ministry, and his answer was positive. And so, here they are.

Of course I am well aware that the poems may not find favour with some critics because they do not carry a readily perceptible 'political punch,' the criterion fashionable these days in some Anglophone quarters for the conferment of the seal of relevance to literature. My humble opinion in this regard is that important and central as politics is in our corporate existence, it should not be the one and only subject matter of our literature. In any case it is not given to just any writer to produce genuinely good political literature. May those capable of pursuing more vigorous committed writing do so; may our radical visionaries bloom. But let there be room for liberal humanists too. The Anglophone story can be told in many ways. To prescribe only politics and proscribe any other subject matter would be to kill our creative spirit, to stultify our imaginative efforts and to truncate our literature.

Although we are a people with a problem, a fact that calls for the accentuation of our condition of marginality, and although when our creative works are examined globally many of us can qualify as committed writers, we do differ in our degree of commitment. Some, because of their heightened level of ideological development, are more engaged, more radical than others. But the dynamism, the vibrancy of Anglophone Cameroon literature cannot be fostered by a spirit that encourages a straitjacket mentality. Neither monolithism nor orthodoxy can be a viable way of life in a world as diverse and complex as ours today.

Just as we meet among the motley crowd in the street the Manichean binarism of the tall and the short, the young and the old, the beautiful and the ugly, the calm and the violent, the radical and the moderate, so do we expect our literature to signalize this diversity in its various forms. Pierre Fandio captures this spirit of our imaginative writing very well when, in an interview with Bate Besong, he affirms that Anglophone Cameroon literature is 'at the same time piercing, incisive, tender, soothing and controversial.' And that is how it should be.

Indeed, as it exists today, our literature reveals a reality we cannot escape from but one that literary critics should rather begin to appreciate: a growth in various directions, a diversity in themes, styles and attitudes, encompassing a wider spectrum of human emotion which is all the more realistic. It is in this context that one can situate *Homage and Courtship;* for it expands the range of human emotion in our literature. Therefore, its publication needs no further justification than that it represents an aspect of the wide-ranging, realistic growth of Anglophone Cameroon literature that objective literary critics must now begin to address.

Shadrach A. Ambanasom
Bambili, Bamenda, Cameroon, July 2007

Foreword

The great subjects of poetry, William Wordsworth wrote, are "the essential passions of the heart" and "the great and simple affections." Consequently, the poet does not become a mere practitioner of artistic craft whose intention is to satisfy the refined taste of a literary connoisseur but one whose "true voice of feeling" as John Keats puts it, is aimed at developing man mentally, physically and spiritually. These views by Wordsworth and Keats (who are among the five major English Romanticists) are indeed the pillars and the heart of Romantic poetry and which, of course, has influenced the Romantic tradition for centuries.

Such palpable influence, whether consciously or unconsciously, is in many ways evident in Shadrach A. Ambanasom's collection of poems titled *Homage and Courtship: Romantic Stirrings of a Young Man*. As the title suggests, the poems are divided into two parts. Part One of the poems pays tribute to patriots and heroes, famous writers, heritage sites, and the natural environment, while Part Two explores the various shades of emotional experience with a beloved who in the poems is identified with the unique figure of Lady Zee. Although the dominant trend in the collection is homage and courtship, the poet expresses concern for other issues like nostalgia or the reminiscences of youth, the passage of time, the brevity of joy, and the human predicament.

The striking force of the poems lies in the intriguing relationship between romanticism and romance. Ambanasom's romanticism is concerned with the concept of nature as a universal being or a cosmic entity, nostalgia, the attempt to link his childhood with the present and the future, and the response to nature at different levels of his development. The poet also demonstrates a penchant for rural subject matter, places and people. In the poet of romance there is a more direct expression of basic human emotions, in particular of love that is enchanting, possessing, seductive, and alluring. We find in the poems, love that is reciprocal and imbued with constancy and understanding.

The poet's fascination for Lady Zee is exceeding. Lady Zee becomes the symbol of beauty, a celebration of beauty. She appears in almost all the poems dealing with courtship as an example of exquisite beauty, or to use the poet's expression "beauty beyond compare". She is to the poet "my lily", "my goddess", "my idol", "my superstella", a summation of Greek and African gods and goddesses. She is the woman whose smiles are capable of transforming sadness to joy, and dullness to liveliness. She is the woman who bridges the gap between romance and romanticism because with her there is a fulfilled union with the rest of the universe including the stars and the clouds. Indeed, in the poet's vision she is the "queen of the universe", an embodiment of all that is glorifying in the universe.

The poems, therefore, articulate a variety of genuine feelings and sublime emotions expressed with sturdy imagery, potent symbolism, and the resonance of sound and rhythm which create a staccato effect in the verse. Of course, the reader will find the poems not only pleasurable to read but will also participate emotionally, intellectually and spiritually in the rich experiences of romance and romanticism that overflow the banks of the poet's imagination.

John Nkemngong Nkengasong
Writer and Critic University of Yaounde 1

PART I

HOMAGE

ABENDONG

Discordant sounded the music of the spheres;
the sun spun around the other planets;
graves and tombs stood gaping, devoid of their
shrouded lodgers; and Harmony onto
Chaos and Melancholy ceded his
cherished throne when Zacharias Abendong
from the world closed his eyes and breathed his last.

Compared to the sustained lamentation
that rose from the souls of Dudum people
to the heavens above and moved the angels,
Niobe over her beloved six sons and six daughters,
merely sighed when the incensed god
put them to death, and Aeneas never wept
at all when his lover, Dido, he lost.

Darkness and chaos hold sway
over the doomed Dudum folk who
grope about and break their necks for
want of light since forever their sun has set.
In their anguish and misery, they curse the
hand that dealt the fatal blow
which left them without a leader.

Wild and deformed have since grown flowers
in his garden, which lacking his tender care,
have followed more the barbaric course
than that for which he'd intended them.
Their ugly shapes would draw tears
even from the hardest of hardened hearts.

3

ONE YEAR OLD

When, with the consent of Hymen,
I broke through my spouse's defense line
and led in my invading army,
she suffered a great loss.

But that deity soon negotiated a truce,
and sent us a female olive tree.
Since then, we have lived in peace,
and that peace is now a year old.

Today, we are watering the olive tree
with precious mineral water
so that it may grow healthy and sturdy,
for upon its health depends ours.

Tree of peace, grow and survive us!
Much have you done to keep us
at Hymen's holy shrine,
and much there is to be done still
if intact must remain our conjugal knot.

ALMA MATER

Far from jarring rustic noise,
and nestled in a green meadow
within the precincts of savanna hills,
you are the rippling pool
of bottomless lore imbibed
by the favoured few.

A solicitous mother-hen,
under your protective wings
congregate your tender brood
to whom you dispense norm, care and love,
with malice towards none,
but with charity for all.

Pride of our fatherland,
your name forever is writ in gold,
and for years to come
you will remain the fortress of culture,
a citadel sought by many,
but a haven attained by a few.

Trumpeter of hope, each year
you proclaim tidings of success,
you bring joy and mirth to many a home,
you reconcile child, mother and father,
helping, thus, to make stronger
what God has put together:
the nucleus of the nation!

THE RUINED PALACE

For heaven's sake mason
touch not the broken brick;
nor the sagging ceiling;
no, not even the mossy windows
through which is heard the sad song
of the wailing, whistling wind.
 Leave them as they are.

Leave the mossy, tiled roof
dripping with water
from the misty eye of the sky.
Disturb not the colony of the feathered tribe
in their snug niche beneath the roof.
Leave them alone, leave them.

Let the spiral staircase,
broken as it is, remain as it is.
Add neither nail nor wood;
leave the balustrade rough and rickety.
Add neither polish nor paint.
Leave them as they are, leave them.

You kill in curing the wound,
but leaving him flayed,
you give the patient long life.
Graft not poison onto his body.
Leave the Palace in its state of decay.
The ruins speak of greater beauty
than you know of;
they speak of the glory of the past;
they speak of an age
that is all but smothered
by a botched civilization,
drowning the ceremony of innocence.

In its mourning garb
the Palace is weeping to quit
an alien century whose values
have gone awry, with the ineluctable
advance of crimes, chaos and greed.
Lift not, lift not the fallen stone.
Leave it, yes, leave it alone.

THE SKY WEEPS

It weeps,
the sky weeps outside;
it weeps with the soft soothing sound
of the gentle pre-dawn rain
as it drops lightly on plantain leaves,
invoking the yester-years of my life,
while snug in bed I muse.

And they flow,
the early years of my life roll on;
they come rushing with a fascinating
vista, teasing me to follow
a young man
on a sentimental trip
down a rusty path of the past.

And they flow,
the days of my past roll on;
they come unfolding
a compelling scenery,
cajoling me to join a teenager
on a safari tour of the past.

Oh yes, they come,
the early days of my life roll on;
they come beckoning me
to follow a toddler
on an emotional journey
down memory lane.

Still it weeps;
the sky continues to weep outside;
it weeps with the mellow music

and the insistent rhythm
of the August morning rain,
summoning the yester-years of my life,
while abed I'm lost in reverie.

Then away with my alter egos I fly;
I fly away with them.
I fly from the harsh present;
I flee to seek solace in my ivory tower,
cuddled in the warm bosom of my grand mother.

THE MEDIATORS

When the new dance arrived,
so tempting and intoxicating was
the rhythm of its music that
the people went wild with excitement.

So the new musicians beat their instruments
and the people danced in the cities
and they danced in the provinces
and they danced in the villages
to the rhythm of this fresh music.

But skeptics and cynics only sneered
at the new dancers who, they said,
were mere experts in adulteration,
putting an end to the high old standards
of their original rhythm.

Now when musicians play a synthetic tune,
and the living respond with complex steps
to the rhythm of soul-elevating melody,
I dance in my heart,
and you dance in your heart,
and we all dance in our hearts
because we are the flexible mediators
of the past and the present,
and hence we are the survivors.

4 WAYS TO DISPATCH YOURSELF

First do not waste time with any Fanta.
You would become but a water drinker.
This is a drink fit only for women
And not meant to touch the lips of pure men.

Secondly with water now discarded,
You should start with palm wine concentrated.
To do this, quaff large jugs of dry potent
Palm wine possessing superior content.

Thirdly, you should guzzle beer or bellevie
For satisfaction and great energy!
Again let these be in huge quantities.
Pay attention to their high qualities.

Fourthly, for quick results, neglect your health
And drain shorts of gin, ignoring your death
For what signifies a little blunder
If you can become a famous fuddler?

HOARDED IMPRESSIONS

They are tender elephant grass
cropped and roughly chewed
by the evening goat
and stored in the stomach
for later pleasant cud-chewing.

They are red wines and spirits
brewed with care but stowed away
in the deep cellars,
that grow in strength and taste
with the passage of time.

They are carved works of art,
fashioned with care and skill,
cheaper when new,
but that grow in value and beauty
with the passage of time.

They are sweet seductive dreams
by the fireside
when we have grown hoarse and grey,
when an old tune rekindles in us
sensations sweet and a return to the past,
since they are now few and far between.

Such are our hoarded impressions
that grow sweeter with the passage of time:
these are our childhood recollections
that become more precious
the closer we get to our sunset.

ICON AND BEACON

Our brilliant icon and beacon,
our candle is out!
An ENSABIAN iroko has fallen,
leaving frightened flora and fauna unprotected;
the ENSAB landscape has thus diminished,
becoming an endangered habitat at the mercy of ogres.

Our brilliant icon and beacon,
our candle is out!
Like sheep without shepherd,
we grope about in the dark;
for a glory has vanished from the face of our earth.

This doom, our gloom, means that
we are not likely to see again,
for a long time to come,
the likes of Babila John Njingum.

Our brilliant icon and beacon,
our candle is out!
Oh yes, a visionary splendour
has faded away from the face of Bali land,
for Bah Njingum has made his final bow,
his exit, and left for that distant country
whose border none can twice traverse.

But in departing,
Dr. Babila has left us a strange parcel;
he has bequeathed to us
bizarre goods parcelled in
parched tongues, drawn faces and tearful eyes.

Willy-nilly, sooner or later,
dear mourners, brothers and sisters,
it will be our turn
to answer our final call.

But will you and I be found
worthy by Him who created us all?
Let us meditate on that.
Death is the unique factor that,
despite laurel wreath or wealth,
levels us all.

Ask not, therefore, for whom the bell tolls.
It tolls not for him alone;
it tolls for you;
it tolls for me;
it tolls for all of us,
the tragic fate of humanity.

Our brilliant icon and beacon,
our candle is out!

THE TALENTED THREE

They came,
they dazzled,
they mesmerized
and, like meteorites,
they have vanished in a flash.

Yes, Bate Besong, Ambe and Gwangwa'a,
Anglophone luminaries
of the dramatic art, have
concluded their noble act on the stage of life.

They came,
they dazzled,
they mesmerized
but, above all,
they shocked all.

Yes, BB, Ambe and Gwangwa'a,
Anglophone dramatic icons,
have left the stage with a bang!
And what a bang!

Yes, BB bowed out with a bang
when, in the company of his
comrades in death, at Edea,
he left us in a dramatic flash
in the sad hour of the collision of the
titanic twain, with a twist of tragic irony.

Oh yes, they came,
they dazzled,
they mesmerized,
but the talented three shocked us

15

when, within a split second,
they bowed to death,
leaving behind but their
decapitated bodies, with their brains
scattered in the wind to inspire humanity.
'A terrible beauty is born.'

EBANG IROKO

The Ebang iroko has fallen,
leaving frightened flora and fauna unprotected;
the Ebang landscape has diminished,
becoming an endangered habitat at the mercy of all.

Our brilliant icon and beacon,
our candle is out.
Like sheep without shepherd,
we grope about in the dark;
for a glory has vanished
from the face of our earth.

The gloom, the doom, means that the benighted Ebang
folk are not likely to see again
the likes of our beloved departed
for a long time to come.

Oh yes, a visionary splendour
has faded away from the face of our earth;
for M.A. Asenek has made
his exit, his final bow, and left for the distant country
whose border none can twice traverse,
bequeathing to us bizarre goods
parceled in parched tongues
drawn faces and tearful eyes.

But sooner or later, willy-nilly
dear brothers and sisters,
it will be our turn
to answer our final call;
for such is the unique factor
that, despite laurel wreath or wealth, levels us all.

THE DREADFUL MONSTER

Let us not talk of yesterday
sweet and palatable though it was
but which now is a dream
vanished at the dawn of today,
and today a skeletal present
full of aching hearts
and sore, wasted bodies,
bodies that barely breathe
while they live in their yester-years.

Let us dwell but on today's anguish
when a giant with a deadly cudgel
bestrides the globe and
bludgeons to death mankind's brightest;
when a merciless monster
is on the rampage
causing havoc and global carnage,
and with a cold, deadly touch devastates
homes and decimates villages,
leaving in his wake pungent putrid flesh and
threatening the extinction of our dusky race.

Let us talk of today's eternal,
solemn toll of funeral bells
and the mournful dirges and elegies
one hears everywhere
or the endless funeral processions
and the countless coffins and floral caskets
one beholds here and there,
making undertakers, for mere lucre, believe
happy days are here to stay.

Let us talk of today's solution,
for in today's talk lies tomorrow's hope.
Let us talk of how to contain this ogre
and chase away grief from the heart
and wipe away tears from the eyes
and rekindle a smile
on the orphan's face
and restore hope to humanity.

A PLEA FOR MERCY

Within a second at your decision
we will all cease to be God's own creation.
The whole world now exists at your mercy.
We earnestly pray for your sympathy.

Like two titans of equal lethal power
with mortal blows you threaten each other.
May God stop you from pressing those buttons
that would put an end to man's existence.

God's flood nonetheless spared a faithful Noah,
but your mortal blow would spare not 'un noir',
since whether from the cold East to the West
or from Uncle Sam's West to the cold East,
not safe is our in-between continent.

Do not wipe out with deadly nuclear power
what God vowed not to destroy with water,
sealing that divine oath with a rainbow.
If in God you trust, then to Him stoop low!
For before God every nation shall bow.

THE GOLDEN MEAN

When Belzebub blew his fiery trumpet,
all his legion rose in arms against God
and they're now trapped in an infernal net;
so are many a brave African god.
There are always present some radical
elements in each human society.
Change, unless rational and practical,
often threatens public security.
However, in order that 'one smash hit'
leads not the world astray, change we all need.
But gradually we have to effect it
if we defend stability indeed.
Chaos is born of radicalism;
darkness, off-spring of conservatism.

THE TALLEST IROKO

In the centre of a forest I stand.
Giant of all greenness, I permit no
other tree to share my height, none at all.
For sustenance I dally not on the
shallow surface of the earth but drive deep
my powerful tap root to the earth's centre.

By sending deep my tap root I have since
discovered with joy what layers of soil
lie hidden in the bowels of the earth
rather than follow 'wise advice' and die
unnoticed on the bankrupt, dry surface,
the realm of herbs, shrubs and common flower.

Tortuous is the way my root passes through;
sometimes it breaks through rocks and waddles through
mud; but it oft wades through healthy water.
Occasionally, it stumbles over
and sustains a dislocation but picks
itself up with buoyancy and goes on.

The deeper it goes the more exquisite
the food obtained; my appetite is
not cloyed by over sweetness,
for sweeter sweetness comes with deeper depth.
Because of the quality of my diet,
I have become the tallest Iroko.
Even as I speak, my root is at work
to make me still the tallest Iroko.

THE CHANGED GROVE

Beloved grove of my wandering infancy
with a heavy heart I return to you,
a grief-stricken grown-up in search of some
clues to unearth comforting memories of
a past that is from me forever gone.

'Tis hard to say how often I roved here
as an unbridled, carefree pre-school lad.
I had measured out my youthful life with
countless rural walks along the verdurous
paths of this memorable childhood haunt.

But oh how changed! Oh how different it is
from that of yest' years clad in rich foliage.
Gone are some of the trees that on this spot
stood with leafy shade as a canopy
over this once dappled path, my tho'oughfare.
Partly gone is the green and dovetailed vault
which would shut the sky from my curious eye.

Everything I knew is either now dead
or has passed from green to maturity.
I'm no exception, growing from a thoughtless
youth to a pensive adult who hears in
the howling wind among the trees above
my head, the mournful moaning of mankind.

CONVERSATION WITH MY HORSE

'My nimble courser how swiftly you fly!
Quickly have I attained eight and twenty
but when I look back at the doors passed by
no laurels for him soon to be thirty;
Keats, Byron and Shelley all reached their height
ere to this door you brought them, who died young.
At door twenty-eight I've got to alight
but my host to entertain with no good song.'
«My green rider, know that many a bard
can yet be made beyond an early door;
some, like you, must first labour very hard,
though gifted others in this are not poor.
Few are the troubadours born geniuses,
but many are transmuted by themselves.»

A WISE DWARF

Long ago, far back in history,
so we are told according to the story,
there lived a famous Fon in Dudum.
His name, as we are told, was Fon Ukum.

Happily did Ukum rule over his people.
He was the coiner of many a riddle.
Never defeated in an argument,
Fon Ukum was wise in his judgment.

People called him second King Solomon.
By this sub-title he was all over known.
But did Ukum this epithet deserve?
No answer but my comment I reserve.

Then Fon Ukum soon received a shock
when his subjects him began to mock
that there was a man wiser than the Fon.
But this was not Ukum's idea of fun.

Who could be this man wiser than the king?
Except for one gift he wasn't worth a thing.
He was Ayari, the dwarf in size;
it seemed he was born only to be wise.

When he heard this, Fon Ukum became angry,
for he had never dreamed of such a story.
He was determined to defeat this man.
So Ukum went ahead to invent a plan.

Yes, there once lived a dwarf in Dudum.
He was well known for his wisdom
in answering any hard question.

To disgrace him was the Fon's intention.
Ayari was the Fon's head to shave
if he considered himself wise and brave.
To the palace he was called one day,
and for his job he was offered no pay.

But let us leave here our famous Fon
and talk more about a dwarf's son.
For his plan Ayari roasted some corn
while the attendants blew the Fon's horn.

Ayari the dwarf knew the Fon's aim
and was bent on destroying the Fon's fame.
Many curious people were there that day
to witness the dwarf have his say.

Ayari gave the Fon some corn to eat
while His Highness' head he shaved on his feet.
And when the Fon's head he had shaved,
the Fon his corn had consumed.

Then the Fon laughed at the wise man
who had been caught in the Fon's plan.
'Make my hair stand on its old spot
if in shaving you are a good shot.'

All the people praised the Fon's wisdom;
yes, all the subjects in his fondom.
'Put back my grains of corn in their old place
if you're the wise Fon of this palace,'
Ayari retorted in the Fon's face.

All were sad that the Fon was conquered
by a dwarf they thought had blundered.
The Fon was distressed and gloomy

as he went about sullen and moody.
He vowed not to bite a morsel
until the dwarf he could muzzle.
He then began another strategy
to salvage his damaged dignity.

Meanwhile our dwarf had returned to his hut,
feeling satisfied and unhurt.
Many to admire him there went,
yes, to a house not better than a tent.

Let us now return to the Fon's second plan,
for truly he was an ill-fated man.
A he-goat was what he gave the pigmy,
and to nurse it well would be his duty.

He charged the midget with these words:
'In the future you'll bring me its young ones.'
The dwarf could be seen on the road
as he walked home with the royal goat.

All the time he thought of the Fon's plan
and then knew what to do, this wise man.
To humiliate the Fon was his aim
and destroy forever the Fon's fame.
How can the Fon give me a he-goat
and expect young ones from such a beast?
How can young ones be produced by a male
unless such an animal is female?

Then Ayari went ahead to work,
for he was not your common jerk.
So he began to cut a log of wood
that would be his answer, and it was good.
Now the peeved Fon happened to pass by

27

and so he asked Ayari the dwarf why
he was hacking off the dead branch of wood.
I say Ayari's response was good.

This is what he said to the king:
'My Lord, I am cutting this thing
because I want to relieve my father
who is labouring to be delivered.'

Sneering, the Fon thundered, 'Oh my wise man,
how can a child be born by a man?',
stupidly forgetting his he-goat,
let every reader of this take note.

Now listen to the dwarf's crushing answer.
He truly proved himself a man wiser:
'If a man can't bear forth children,
why expect young ones from your he-goat then?'

To talk of Fon Ukum's ignominy
would need more space and another story
which I have no time to tell.
Readers, here ends my simple tale.

BREVITY OF JOY

One gloomy afternoon when low-spirited,
I know not why,
my soul to cheer with music
I decided, and Paul Mauriat was my artist.

And when his instrumental liquid notes
on my ears began to drop,
I was transported on the wings of Fancy
to the land of blissful ease.

There, my friends and relatives came,
tumbling around me.
In various moods they fell:
the quick and the dead,
some accusing and weeping,
others clinging onto me,
and refusing to let me go.

Never to quit that land I vowed.
Gradually, the clime changed:
The seasons, vegetation and the fauna,
like the people, lazily passed by,
vying with one another for a place in my soul.

But while I was thus contented
with them to dwell forever,
behold stark reality struck!
And a sudden electronic click I heard.

And then, the people and the birds,
the trees and the animals,
the clime and the vegetation,

were at a standstill,
and a moment later, all disappeared,
leaving my soul swelling with sensations sweet
and a mind musing on the brevity of joy.

ON LOSING MY HAIR

In vain pages of journals
have I turned over and over.
Bootless some scientific annals
perused with anxiety and in anger
in an attempt to discover
the treatment for a balding head.

Fruitless my efforts with doctors
(personal contact or letters)
to halt the insidious invaders
of my receding forehead.

While pondering over this at home one day
I raised my drooping head and
saw near me Julius Caesar of Rome
with little hair on his own head
but gallant green laurels he wore instead
which have since immortalised him.

Close behind Caesar stood Shakespeare
the great English dramatic poet,
whose crown was bereft of hair,
but garlanded with green leaves.

Inspiration I drew from this pair:
Never to while away useful time
in talking away all my hair,
but labouring hard on my books
so that, like theirs, when my hair
falls off, laurels take its place,
in spite of wrinkles and lost looks.

THE HORSE RIDER

Majestic bronze horse, stiff-necked must he be
who, passing near-by, would not cast on you
a second glance;
what masterpiece is here
displayed to feast the eyes of art lovers!

On your back is a brave bronze rider,
on his left flank a thick-jewelled scabbard,
and a raised and poised spear in his right
hand, about to pin down,
I know not, what tyrant.

Happy is the dauntless Bamoun warrior
borne by such a peerless, dazzling stallion.
Rearing on your stout hindlegs,
with your graceful forelegs in the air,
you seem ready to vault over
a perilous fence.

Tell me, magic horse, where you're flying to
with this intrepid fighter.
Who is it that has incensed his anger?
I will call your rider Promethus unchained;
I will also call him Toussaint L'Ouverture,
sent to liberate mankind chafing in bondage.

INDIFFERENT NATURE

When the hungry vagrant got to the mango-tree,
its branches were drooping with full load,
and ripe mangoes emitted a fragrance
that watered his mouth and
kept murmuring bees buzzing busily.

Instinct drew him to the ripe and juicy fruit.
And with his hunger's edge blunted, he now saw
that among the ripe mangoes that lay under
the tree were fruit with bleeding stalks.

But there had been no wind,
and no storm had invaded the tree
when both ripe and green fell,
an act of indifferent Nature.

If the ripest must fall first, as they say,
how come the untimely fall of the green fruit
whose stalks were yet fresh with life's latex
fit to rebuff the buffets of life?

Shaken was the pensive tramp
by the conclusions of his musings:
His own precarious existence, he perceived,
was an accident in the palm of inscrutable Nature.

THE DUDUM CITIZEN

The flowers that bloom at dawn and die at noon
warn us of the passing time since our birth,
how at our journey's end we are all soon
to arrive to bow down before cold death.
The plants that rot leave behind a few seeds
to multiply and continue their kind.
All humans count among their various needs
the strong desire to propagate mankind.
The beautiful rose dies that is healthy
but is not heard of if it leaves no trace
to show to the world its glorious beauty
that would have been the subject of much praise.
The clean, productive Dudum citizen
who dies, even poor, won't be forgotten.

THE CAGED LION

He was her pet lion.
Like a kitten she nurtured him,
feeding him with crumps of meat
from her own hand, the harmless cub
she had picked up in the park
when his parents by a poacher had been shot.

He grew up with her other pets
and with her kitten and lap-dogs.
The young naturalist fed him from her
own china; but as he grew into a bigger
lion, the European blonde
could not take chances.
So in her iron cage she confined him.

There she fed him with rats, moles and beef;
for though domesticated, he remained
true to his nature; blood and not herbs
was his native diet, and on that he lived.
Thrice a day the woman fed him for
many years-morn, noon and eve.

The African villagers admired her skill
in handling the tame lion as he voraciously
devoured his meal with a smouldering,
terrifying fire in his eyes.
Then it happened: one fateful eve
the blonde was found gored to death near the cage
with the lion at large.

Don't go searching for this lion in the wild.
In vain would you find him there;
for there is one in each man.

Each man nurses in his inside
his own domesticated lion,
his own smouldering fire,
caged up by norms, lore and mores.
Fear then, the fire in each man!
Beware of each man's caged lion!

THE LAST SALUTE

In his early days
he had won souls for his Creator.
To conclude in style the task he had begun,
he was determined to live.
Alas! that job he never lived to complete.

On his sick-bed, a sinister shadow
could be discerned creeping steadily
over his afflicted body, and gradually
overrunning a terrain that was ours.

When he had to put to sea,
David Achomba ordered the oars be cleaned
and his boat unmoored
before he went down into it
with no remorse expressed.

Down the gently flowing river,
that noble fellow was borne
in the incense-perfumed vessel
heading for the distant land
whose boundary none can twice traverse.

With an up-raised hand, in a final salute,
and with godlike grit,
he shed no tears,
he voiced no curse,
he expressed no fears
when he finally crossed the bourn.

On the misty shore we stood, lead-footed,
with bleeding hearts,
partially blinded by salty water.
And with a mutilated dirge,
we shuffled home, drenched by tears from a weeping sky.

ELEMENTAL FURY

When I hear the rain pounding on my roof
and then pattering on the window pane,
when the trees swing in the dark,
and creak under the force of the storm,
I fear the forces of nature are around.

When lightning flashes and thunder roars
and men fall down to avoid the blow,
when a thunderbolt breaks the ribs of men
and dismembers them limb by limb,
I fear the elements of fury are unchained.

When I hear in the howling of the wind
and in the drumming of Dudum Falls
the wailing of bereaved mothers,
and the groan of separated lovers,
I fear the agents of doom are at large.

Then secure in my world within
I reinforce my doors and thank
my ancestors for the calm
that reigns in my homestead,
invoking them to instill in my
slumbering inmates and me sounder sleep
so that we may know nothing
of the elemental fury
that has gripped the world without.

A GRAIN OF CORN

Bernard Ambanasom, my son Bernard,
your untimely death
shook and shattered the very depth
of my existence, knocking down, for a while,
the pillars of my faith.

Since then my life has never been the same.
But, thanks to God's healing power, my
faith in Him was rekindled and reinforced.
And now, in the Lord, my faith again is strong.

Bernard, my son, ten years have gone by
since you departed from us.
Ten years have rolled on
since you succumbed to the
lethal weapon of a traitor.

Oh murder most foul and most traitorous!
Murder most heinous and unspeakable!
Yes, sonny, you were cut down by
the treacherous weapon of
one in whose care you had been entrusted,
one in whose custody you felt most secure.

Alas, my son, that traitor, your school teacher!
A man may smile and smile,
and yet be a devil!
Cruel man, your name is villainy.

Bernard, my son, ten years have passed on
and you are still with us.
Indeed, you will never die.
So long as we breathe God's serene air,
so long as we draw sustenance

from His bountiful earth,
so long as we plant and we harvest,
so long as we consume and propagate
your eternal grain of corn,
you will continue to live with us.

Precocious son of the soil,
unknown to you, at the tender age of 8
you had sown the seed of your immortality.
Oh yes, Bernie, thanks to that
brown grain of corn planted by your
innocent hand in our homestead,
and though you tasted not of your labour,
that grain, today sustains us all
and keeps your memory alive.

Each grain of brown corn
now planted and harvested,
each grain of brown corn
now eaten and propagated,
each grain of brown corn
now sold or offered to God
by our family, comes from that
original grain your tender
hand had planted before
your bright and promising flame
was snuffed out.

Your grave in Baforkum cemetery
has since become a permanent feature
of the local landscape;
your final resting place in a country
church yard has become our family shrine
and the motive for our yearly pilgrimage
to renew our wreaths and pledges,
to commune and fellowship with you in spirit.

Thus a decade has expired
since our first pilgrimage.
For ten years we have visited this shrine.
Ten years have passed by
since you passed away.
But, thanks to a grain of corn,
you continue to live; besides,
to God we commended your soul.

That you are in Abraham's bosom,
we doubt it not, son.
We pray you to intercede for us, poor sinners.
As for your poisoner, well,
to the Almighty God
belongs the ultimate verdict.
May His name be glorified.

HEALING DREAMS

Great pals we were;
wherever I was, there you were.
At the dining table or in the shower,
like birds of a feather,
we were spotted together.

Little wonder, then, that,
following your untimely demise,
I was totally devastated,
reduced to an emotional wreck,
and nearly demented.

For five years I was haunted by your spirit;
for five years I walked like a ghost;
yes, for five years my heart bled painfully.
Deep was the wound inflicted on my heart,
and it was sore and slow to heal.

Yet, those sorrowful years
were also years of joy.
While in the day I grieved over your death,
in the night I rejoiced in my sleep.
I dreamt sweet dreams about you.
For five years, and almost every night,
you visited me in my sleep;
you came to me in my dreams.
I dreamt that you and I were together;
I dreamt sweet dreams about you.
0! a tonic they were, those dreams.
A boon, they were to my soul.

But at the break of day
they would vanish away;
I would rise from sleep in the morning
and cry to dream again;
I would try, in vain, to clutch at those dreams.
They would vapourise into thin air,
but leaving my heart brimming with joy.

Bernard, after five years you stopped coming;
after five years you ceased to visit me.
After five years you refused to appear in my dreams.
Still I longed in vain to dream about you.
Yes, sonny, I pondered about your absence.

I asked myself:
'Where are they gone to, those glorious dreams?
Why don't they come back to me?
Where is he gone to, my beloved son?
Why doesn't he come back to me in my dream?'
I asked myself these and other questions.
Then out of Hades, out of the land of the dead,
a voice spoke out loud and clear:
'Living man,
Listen to the voice of the Lord of Hades.
Your innocent and upright son came here.
Because of his moral rectitude
and good works on earth,
he was granted one wish of his choice.
And he opted to return to earth
to mend his father's broken heart.
But since once dead, no one ever
leaves Hades in flesh and blood,
Bernard was offered the medium of
the dream to access you for the period of five years.

'So, for five years he came to you in your dreams;
for five years he visited you in your sleep;
for five years he came to keep you company;
for five years he came to assuage your pain,
soothe your soul and make you happy.

'That joy kept you healthy.
That comfort sustained your life.
That happiness healed your heart.
With your cardiac wound completely cured,
Bernard considered his mission accomplished.
So, after five years, he was quickly
called back to the Underworld
to prepare for his transition to Heaven.'

Thus spoke the Lord of Hades,
leaving my heart flowing with sensations sweet
and a mind teeming with happy thoughts of
my son in Heaven.

WATCH YOUR APPETITE

There is a thin thread of family fat
Running through our blood stream.
Its origins are the genes of ancestors.
It poses a serious threat to family health
And my duty is to expose it and to
Alert the Family to its pernicious power.
But the environment plays a big role too.

Eat light, drink smart;
Drink smart to feel light.
Eat not late at night.
Eat intelligently to reduce
Your incidence of coronary thrombosis,
For upon this depends your life.

Your heart is a terrible thing to destroy.
The fear of food and drink is the
Beginning of the loss of weight.
It makes sense to keep down your weight.
It pays to control your appetite,
For upon this depends your life.

Exercise is a sure way
To shed unwanted pounds.
Jogging is the way to lose excess kilos.
Exercise and control your appetite.
Consider this and mend your ways,
For upon this depends your life.
If you must drink,
Do so in strict moderation.
It hurts to be a drunk.
There is nothing but misery
In a life of alcoholism.

Its nefarious effects are tragic blunders,
Dishonour and domestic disasters,
Giving rise to obloquy and regret.

Therefore, today, your happiness should
Reside in an occasional, healthy sip
In a general, disciplined life of
Reading, hard work and sobriety.
Consider this and mend your ways,
For upon this depends your life.

THE GENUINE SCHOLAR

(To Professor Paul Mbangwana)

He appears hungry;
but his heart hungers not for food.
That is the look of a scholar!
He needs knowledge; he wants to know.
He seeks to scale higher heights to harvest
shining stars, and to fathom deeper depths
to extract precious gems for our delight.

While the rest of humanity is asleep,
he is awake, anxious about its fate,
and, like a bee seeking for nectar,
he is scaling mountains for their honey;
he is awake, digging deep deeper depths
to unearth hidden wealth
to enrich impoverished humankind;
he is awake, worried at improving
the lot of his kind on worrying Mother Earth.

He is the true benefactor of man.
He is Mbangwana Paul.
That is the genuine scholar!

ODE TO SABGA HEIGHTS

1

Sabga! Twenty-one long years have gone by!
Sabga la plus belle, a score and a year
Have rolled away and I am here again!
Lying between Bambili and Bamessing
You'll always be Nature's gift to mankind,
Breathtaking beauty to gladden his soul.
Not for nothing are your great formations
Which constitute geological marvels.
Not in vain was created your colourful
Landscape, a boon to native or alien.

2

Arousing are the fluctuating contours
Of the rise and fall beat of your vista.
Sabga, you are Nature's own perfect poem
Destined to inspire all the potential poets.
Sabga, you are the fountainhead or the
Creative spring of some of my own lyrics.
Thus not for nothing do I value you
Nor in vain do I muse or meditate
On you; for though distant from you, many
a benefit have I derived from you.

3

Oh Sabga, one need not be a genius
To fancy that to access the Poetic Hall
Of Fame, the immortal Wordsworth passed here too.
For in you are found some of those features
That defined his pastoral existence.
One is tempted to venture that this is

The same or, at least, the spiritual haunt
Of his glorious and robust, rustic life:
There is his vale and that is his tall rock;
There is his cataract and that is his hill;
There is his mountain and that is his dell;
There is his shepherd and that's his cottage.
Yonder are his huge majestic boulders,
All of which are geological wonders
To arrest briefly the breath of both the brute
And the cultured, the rude and the polite.

4

In your wild ugliness lies your beauty;
Your glory lies in your savage splendour.
There are undulating hills with dotted
Flat tops here and there; scrub land and dwarfish
Vegetation punctuate your surface too.
But also present is arable land,
Isolated patches of lush verdure,
Source of food for folk from time immemorial,
interspesed with flora and fauna.

5

From Bambili to Bamessing on your
Right, or from Bamessing to Bambili
On your left, is a forbidding, massive
Mountain of a rock lying like a planet
Close to the road and stretching very high
Into the sky and reminding viewers
Of their puny nature in the face of
Its eternal subduing power. Opposite
It, in the distance, and above the vale,
Runs down the sparkling, sounding cataract.

6

Sabga! land of ambient, romantic ease!
Oh wondrous landscape, haunt of poets and tourists!
What great force created you? What fire, what steam?
What compulsive power from the earth's centre
Brought about all this magnetic scenery?
To look at its fantastic handiwork
Nature itself must be smiling right now;
Yes, for its masterpiece is here indeed.
Your panoramic view and volcanic
Cones, coupled with other geological
Features, compel your lovers to ponder
And wonder at your creation and Creator,
Winning, sometimes, from among the heathen,
A soul for the Son of your great Creator.
Behind your being must be a mightier Being.

7

Sabga, for more than twenty years you've been
To me a mental retreat and comfort.
You have been my spiritual pilgrimage
And a moral force inducing good deeds,
My psychological refuge and, in
Class, my pedagogic inspiration.
If all our planned visits to you have failed,
All my imaginary trips have taken place
And will continue to do so till death.

8

Sabga, man's worst enemy is man himself.
Unless man controls his own appetite,
He will end up destroying you and himself.
Unless man curbs his greed in using your
Resources, you will soon be denuded

While that man is left unprovided for.
Gradual deforestation, harmful work
Of man's hands, speaks of your slow but steady
Death; the dangerous drop in your water
Table spells man's future doom if nothing
Is done to arrest the bad situation.
It makes good sense, therefore, for your greatest
Beneficiary, man, to pay great heed.
He must avoid alien eucalyptus;
He must go for local mahogany.
It is environmentally friendly.
It pays to be conscious of Mother Earth:
The environment and nature protection.

9

Despite incipient insecurity
Jeopardizing your idyllic picture,
Despite occasional, nascent hold-ups
Instilling fear in your admirers,
Sabga, I'll continue to adore you.
How can I ever forget to do so?
I will go on worshipping you for what
You have done, been and will continue to
Be to me. Indeed, I love you even
More now for what you are to Lady Zee
Who, in her little, beautiful cell phone,
Has stored countless pictures of your features,
Depicting your striking capricious moods,
Food for the future and restoration
Of her own sensitive romantic soul.

PART II

COURTSHIP

GO & TELL LADY ZEE

Blow! Zephyr blow!
Blow my message away!
Carry my words and whisper
them into the ears of Lady Zee
Tell my Rose among the maidens
that April is here
and I am waiting
waiting for her.

Go! Zephyr go!
Carry my words away!
Tell my Lily among the thorns
that gone is the harmattan,
gone the season of pain,
that April is here
healthy April, April of shoots and buds
and that I am waiting
waiting for her.

Float Zephyr float! Float and
tell the melon of my eye
that in this month of the year
(when fresh are buds with dew
and healthy the air breathed by all as
tourists long to travel far and beyond
to savour the sweetness of the air)
yes, tell the melon of my eye
that I am waiting, anxiously waiting for her.

MY SUPERSTELLA

You are my superstar
which, on a starry night,
shines brightest in the sky.
For, when from your habitual spot
you appear in the heavens,
you eclipse, at once, lesser stars
that peep timorously from under
your powerful beam
to find inferior roles for themselves.

You are my superstella, sans pareil.
Yet, for all your rare endowments
that place you in a class all alone,
you are most modest and mature;
you remain sober and refuse to be
intoxicated by the force of your charms;
you resist letting your brains and beauty
go to your head like potent palm wine
to pollute your reason.

You are my shining star.
My wish is that you may continue
to shine on me with the constancy
and grace that make you Duty's dearest daughter
and kindle in me the spark that will
engrave your name in the Hall of Fame
as a brilliant belle, but self-effacing.

HER SMILES

When Lady Zee's smiles change dull Septembers
Into joyous and fruitful Decembers,
Then the pangs felt in the rainy season
Are healed by the balms of the dry season;
So birds, beasts and men who have been hiding
From the season's roughness come out singing
To praise God, everyone, for His kindness
In changing dullness into happiness.
Who, unless a dead man, can fail to feel
This important change with much hope and zeal?
That is how my heart feels when your great hips,
Coupled with those smooth and delicious lips,
Drive away all darksome clouds from your face
And dress it with a cheerful look of grace.

WE ARE ONE

You dwell with me, my darling;
you walk with me all the hours of the day.
Hardly does an hour pass by
that I do not meditate on you.

I dream of you, my dear;
I dream of you all the nights of the year.
Not a single night goes by
but I must muse upon you.

True, you stay far away,
and apart from me;
yet you live nigh enough
to be a part of me.

There is no severance
of the bond binding us;
for our two souls are one,
made of invisible elastic.
And although it might be overstretched, it would suffer
no rupture;
for we are one.

BEAUTY BEYOND COMPARE

When I meditate on sweet Zee
of a Monday morning, a fortnight ago,
as she awaited, by the bus, the approaching
hour of her departure on vacation,
a figure glorious and ethereal to behold,
with vitality in her eyes,
with bright, fresh and delicate lips
complementing a chocolate haunting face,
with smooth, soft and well-kept hands,
a shape resplendent, irresistible and intensely desirable
in a pink attire that proclaimed her
queen of the universe, I cannot but grant
that she is a beauty beyond compare;
that hers is the kind of captured beauty that lasts forever;
that, indeed, 'Beauty is truth, truth beauty.'

HAPPY VALENTINE'S DAY

On this day
When lovers feel great
To be loved and to be truly in love;

On this Lovers' day
When lovers young and old
Are united by the youthful
Spirit of Love
Moving all over the world;

On this very romantic day
When Venus the goddess of love
Is moving in hearts bound together
By her son's arrows,
By arrows from Cupid's bow,
Stirring and inspiring lovers to scribble
Words of endearment to beloved ones;

Oh yes, on this Valentine's day
My thoughts fondly fly to the shrine
Where lives my idol, my goddess,
Reminding her that the flames ignited
More than three years ago
Are still burning with as much
Power as when first set ablaze;
That the fuel's fountain is still full.

It could not have been otherwise;
The sweet girl I set eyes on
More than three years ago is just
As wonderful and gracious now as then;
She is just as beautiful and attractive
Now as then.
By the same token my love for her
Is just as constant as ever!
Happy Valentine's Day, Lady Zee.

ON MEETING LADY ZEE

Dear Zee, when this morning I set eyes
on you, I was simply out of breath
on account of your sensuous outfit:
a brown trico over brown velvet shorts,
revealing a stunning callipygian behind;
while blessed brown slippers kissed your tender feet,
a lucky gold chain lay between your ripe breasts.

Your pretty face haunts me day and night,
while your succulent, scarlet lips are juicy
honeycombs beckoning to be eaten.
If I have fallen, head over heels, for you,
it is because I am beside myself.

Stronger than the strength of the violent storm,
and deeper than the depth of the vast ocean,
are my feelings for you.
I am buffeted in the rough sea of passion,
and will soon sink unless you save me.
You alone hold, in your hand, the life-buoy,
and, thus, the choice whether I flounder or I float.

Could ever a man bare his heart this much
who did not admire genuinely?
Was there ever a love-worn insomniac
without an object in view?
Will you rebuff or will you receive me?

Greater yearning has no devotee than this,
that a youth muses and meditates upon
a girl until he forgets to eat!
Truly, I say unto you, Zee:
With you in mind, these days, my lot is neglect.

A MOMENT AGO

A moment ago,
driving in a pleasure car in dreamland,
and defying gravity, we were ejected,
you and me, by the romantic law of motion,
into the celestial, ethereal region,
way beyond earthly cares.

As we sailed on cotton-white fluffy clouds,
and trailed other glorious clouds,
our two souls soon dissolved into one.
And, like the clouds that gathered and formed
countless designs and burst again,
our single soul assumed numerous
shapes but annihilated them just as fast.

After gleefully floating across the sky,
we landed noiselessly back on earth.
But no sooner were we back to land
than we soared to more romantic sites
where we stood rapt in contemplation
of craggy precipices, dizzy hanging cliffs,
cascading streams, frothing pools, and roaring dells;
or where, on our elbows, we lay supine in
rippling, savanna grass
as the fresh April breeze caressed our temples.
What ecstasy it is for me, Lady Zee,
to fling open the fountain of feelings
inspired by reflections on you!
What soothing and relieving sensations
course through my corporeal frame
when I muse deeply upon you!
Little was I aware of the value
of my hoarded impressions of you.

Now I should know better.
I will garner food for future days
so that, when on long vacation
you will have gone, I will sit back
and, yes, even in fantasy,
see, smell, hear or feel you
as often as I want, to my heart's content,
indeed, for the restoration of body and soul.

A UNIVERSAL TYRANT

Lady Zee, you have rekindled in me
a desire long thought dead,
a fire long believed extinct, and
a spark long considered gone.

In me you have caused a tremor
that has rocked the foundation of my world.
Like a volcano, stirred from within,
and about to erupt, I am on fire,
the very stuff out of which is made
the conflagration of empires,
the passion Paris prior to the capture
of fair Helen must have known.
Indeed, love is a universal tyrant
to whose command all men must succumb.

Of all the girls I have encountered,
all the maidens I have met,
all the fair women I have known,
none has worked on me a spell
as you have done;
nor drawn me out of my shell
as you have done;
nor stirred my imagination
as you have done.

With you in mind, I am a different man.
Even as I struggle to form these words,
propelled by passion and a power beyond me,
I know not what, nor who, I am.

When the day comes that in school
I must see you, my heart rejoices like
the clock-bird, at the dawn of day,
pouring out its soul in a throaty song.

At such moments I experience an
unbelievable pleasant wave of feelings,
a fantastic sensation rippling through
my veins with restorative effects.
This, I would not exchange for a king's crown.

SHE BRIGHTENS ALL

This week the folk have been moaning their fate,
for dark, dull clouds have overrun the sky,
leaving the sun in its incomplete state
in the daily radiance it should supply
when it brightens human life in its sway.
Without it living things will surely die.
Yes, many a man this week is not gay
as everyone utters only a sigh.
But Lady Zee has pitied them today:
She's decided the folk to gratify.
She's risen and pushed all the clouds away
as soon as her smile appeared by and by.
Thus without Zee's smile our day will be dull,
for she's the sun that brightens me and all.

ALL FOR A FACE

Here is the face, Lady Zee's face.
This is the bewitching face
that has beamed on me
and lit my path to self-discovery.
I now put it down in plain words:
Each romantic man is a potential poet
waiting but for the right woman
to ignite a flame in his heart.

There was a time
when to me this haunting face
with its bulging seductive eyes
was the fountain of many a lyric,
the muse that mediated in my moments
of poetic parturition.
My heart still swells with joy
to think that the charming face
can yet kindle and energize.

How sweet it is that,
of all potential poets,
I have been fated to fête this face!
Do I then elope with her?
Do I dare to defy the world?
Can I risk all for a face
and by so doing become a
Paris or a pariah?

A FRUITFUL VOYAGE

Sweet Zee, well have you marked out
the course of your fruitful voyage.
The imaginative English boats are rigged
for a cruising voyage across the oceans:
your alert mind on the way to fictional
adventures is resolutely set.

Sure to sail beyond national waters,
you will be transported by lyrical
vessels to alien realms and kingdoms
with different climes and mores.
Buffeted dramas, stormy epics and rapid, gliding
prose will pilot you to populous ports
and swarming cities. For full are the sails
of the novel, never in want of winds.

The creative crafts will make you discover
foreign folk of diverse deportment:
some will be impulsive, others phlegmatic.
These betray impetuous tantrums
like the angry seas in tempestuous weather;
those reveal stable tempers like the steady ship in calm
waters.
But by and large they remain spirited types
animated by basic human passions
limited to neither time nor place.

The more you traverse the fictive oceans,
the wiser you will become in the ways
of the world; and being a shrewd
student of human nature and literature,
I hope, you will provide your own
locally-rigged vessel with a sterling crew,
exporting for consumption the customs of Cameroon.

FROM GLOOM TO GLEE

With no destination in sight,
and like an errant cloud
at the mercy of whimsical winds,
I rambled on the campus,
with my moods tottering
on the verge of despair.

Then Fate cried out loud and clear:
'Let there be sunshine'
and my heart gave a lurch,
when I caught sight of my heart.
Behold I beheld my goddess!
Behold I bumped into Zee!
Behold I from the brink of
despondency was yanked
onto the terrafirma of hope!

My heart throbbed
and swelled with joy
as I hurried to greet my heart.
Having espied me,
she, in turn, rushed to meet me!

Her tuneful voice was celestial
music in my ear,
and her face a magnet,
ever drawing me closer to her;
while her figure was pure
glory to behold.

Suddenly my condition changed,
as a rain-drenched cock
became a jubilant throaty rooster

announcing the dawn of a brand new day;
and the world that, hither to,
had worn a cloud of gloom,
now put on an apparel of glee.

CELLPHONE CONTACT

Lady Zee, you are the contents of my mind.
You fill every nook and cranny
of my fancy the way
a boiled egg fills its shell,
leaving me, in the night,
to wallow in sweet insomnia.

Thanks to a hi-tech gadget,
we have made nonsense
of the gulf between us,
reducing to nil nine scores and ten miles;
yes, thanks to the magic of a quaint
contraption, we have demolished
that long distance and reached out
to touch each other,
savouring the voice, clutched
to the ear, at the other end.

Yet, for all the marvels of this hi-tech gadget,
I hear but a mere voice!
I crave for more than a disembodied voice;
ours is a love based more on physics and less on
metaphysics,
more on the senses, and less on theory.

For, hearing Zee is believing;
seeing Zee is proof;
but touching Zee is confirmation.
I hope to palpably prove
and confirm your existence
when next I come to town
to hear, see, and touch you.
Then will I believe, prove and confirm your being.

THE SPITTING COBRA

If in the season of romance
I espy Lady Zee with a youth
walking arm-in-arm in love,
or if I find her consorting with her peer
though he may look at her with a leer;

If in the garden of love
I chance upon Zee chatting
with her equal even as
he longs to devour her in lust,
then the spitting cobra in me
will be barely ruffled.

But should I spot her anywhere
in the company of my match,
with or without designs on her,
even as they sit
merely to dream away their time,
then and anon my cobra-head
rears itself forebodingly;

Then and anon my ready fangs are filled
with the blinding gall
that will teach my heedless rival
how to grope his way in the dark
to find his final bed six feet deep.

THE DREAM

Last night I had a very scary dream
In which, to project into the future
Lady Zee's beauty and charms, I cut into
The bark of a mango-tree her sweet name,
Daring my friends to show me her better
If, indeed, in this age they can find one.

With this single act not contented,
In thick blue paint I wrote the same
On the ceiling of my classroom,
Challenging my peers to name
Another girl with natural gifts
Of genius and charms superior to hers.

Still with this second deed less satisfied,
And driven by the urge to proclaim her fame,
I, on my school desk, engraved her name
And also on the bench on which I sat,
Daring my colleagues to produce her equal,
Knowing full well that Zee was sans pareil.

But years later, many years, in that dream,
When I returned to the old wounded tree,
The big one on which I had carved "Zee",
Behold! "Zee" was no where to be found.
The wound had healed up, consuming her name,
Leaving no trace of her behind.

When to the classroom I turned, I was faced
With ruins and total desolation:
Where, on the ceiling her name was writ large,
I beheld a grim, gaping cavity,
A parody of the former ceiling,

With no sign of Zee's name.
Undaunted I made straight for desk and bench
Where with my tool I had engraved her name.
Behold the story was the same:
Bench and desk were all but gone,
Reduced to dust and mud by moth and all
Without a clue of Zee's name.

Dejected, baffled and motionless I stood.
Then a cynical and disembodied voice
Spoke to my hearing in that very dream:
"Puny man, like the foregoing examples,
Your tall, stately Lady Zee will pass away:
Nothing on this earth can dare Time's sickle".

"Impossible! It can't be," I replied,
"If Zee cannot exist in these ways,
she will live forever in my poetry."
When I turned around to see who it was,
I was wide awake, alone in my bed,
While my Lady Zee was far away from me.

THE BEAST IN MY INSIDE

When, under the spell
of Lady Zee's beauty,
I am awash with
a flood of feelings and passion,
then the beast in my inside
swings from side to side
as it strains to break loose
from its leash.

I become weak-kneed
and succumb to its demand.
Then through the walls
of my inside as if
through a paper wall
breaks the impetuous animal.

With incredible speed and ardour
it bolts for its catch,
bounding and leaping
over valleys and mountains,
yapping and whining
over hills and vales.

With fire in its eyes
and desire in its heart
it makes for its target
with this sole craving.
But as it bundles itself up with a
pounding heart prepared to pounce on its prey
With a keen, horny appetite,
behold Lady Zee lifts up
her hand and commands
"No! Stop it!"

Instantly slumps the brute,
helpless and harmless as if
impaled on the spot
with a divine stake.
0! Lady Zee says "no" with such sweet grace
that she pleases even as she refuses;
she attracts even when she rejects!

FUTURE WOMAN OF LETTERS

Dear Zee, with empty hands I come to you,
bringing neither silver nor gold.
But such gifts as I own I give you:
stories from my shelf and songs from my soul.
Such are the presents I drop in your lap
for the improvement of your mind.

For well I know that a well-nurtured mind
is an antidote against darkness, and
a vaccine against ignorance, both of
which push further the frontiers of dumbness.
For, truly I tell you, the human mind
uncultivated, is a terrible thing to waste.

The rapidity with which you devour
my tales and the growing interest you take
in my songs give me reason to believe
in the possibilities of the Cameroonian woman
and the spring of your literary career.
There is, indeed, cause for optimism.

I foresee a great woman in you,
one with awesome oratorical powers
and eloquence unsurpassed.
In you I envision a fine wielder
of the power of the pen, a word-artist.
Perhaps in you is born our own Jane Austen.

Already evident are signs of things to be.
The mustard seed has taken root;
the giant tree will surely come to be.
The girl is mother of the woman to be.
Your felicitous prose and ease of
expression, fruit of your voracious
reading, prefigure the future woman
of letters that my sweet Zee will be.

THE MOSQUITO

The mosquito defiles my coy lady;
the puny insect devours her skin.
The cruel creature leaves its odious
bites on her beautiful body
now in need of a soothing balm.

While my eyes feast on her glorious body,
the mosquito gorges on her.
The wretch takes without wooing what with
persuasion is beyond me.

Do I dare to debauch her?
Do I yield to the id
and call in question civilization?
Should my id take the driver's seat
and drive home the throbbing car?

The Mosquito attacks and violates;
it seizes, sucks and succeeds.
The beast grabs and ravishes my lady
and then abandons her with bleeding scars.
Yea, the brainless brute has an id
to satisfy, but I have an
Ego to defend.

YOU ARE THE BEST

Much have I travelled
and much have I seen
in terms of female beauty and charms.
But never have I met
a girl with your charms.

There's a style in your walk,
and a charm in your smile;
there's magic in your look,
and majesty in your manners,
all of them a magnate
that pulls me to bow down
before you and worship at your feet
and pay tribute to your rare beauty.

What my eye admires
my heart desires.
Yes, my heart hungers after you!
What sensations
when you're in my arms!
Zee, you're the Best!

ZEE IS MY MUSE

My poetry is Zee and Zee my poetry.
Lady Zee was ordained to inspire me
and I fated to celebrate her beauty,
the one the muse, the other the bard.

Without Zee the poet would cease to be,
and sans the poet, unsung would be
Lady Zee's charms.
Thus, for better or for worse,
we are destined to be of service
to each other.

Isn't this what fate is all about?
Isn't this part of Venus's sightless design?
Her blind kid, cupid, with his arrow
has pierced through our hearts,
making it possible for me
to send to Zee another Valentine,
wishing her rapid recovery
from her malaria bout.
Happy Valentine, Lady Zee!

THE MUSE IS STILL THERE

My bardic harvest is meagre
after an apparent lyric drought.
The yield is scarce not
for want of a muse;
no, the poetic product is paltry
because of the delicacy of my Muse's situation.

While active as ever
is my mythopoetic faculty,
stable Ego calls for caution,
restraining zestful Id
to find work with visionary Sublimation.
Best safety, they say, lies in fear.

Now have I realized how
impossible it is for me
to scribble a neutral poetic line
to my Muse; no! no neutrality,
for the Muse is too much with me.
And not for anything in the world
will I dispense with my Muse.
I live, breathe, and muse upon my Muse.

HAPPINESS AND SADNESS

Dear Lady, I cannot enjoy brightness
and suffer you to undergo darkness
when with two or only a simple dime
I can promptly come to your aid in time
and put on your visage a little smile
even if it lasts only for a while,
and by so doing, I your sadness erase,
an act that brightens up your haunting face.
For surely it is my greatest pleasure
to be of service to my dear Treasure.
So, accept, Lady Zee, these pennies few
as a token of my esteem for you.
For incomplete would be my happiness
until you're free from the grip of sadness.

BREATHTAKING BEAUTY

When I was lucky to come across you,
when you charmed me for the first time
with your striking features
and I began to write lyrics to you,
this girl's picture you see is an interpretation
of how you appeared to me then;
this amazing photo in your hands is the way I saw Zee at
the beginning of our relationship;
the very photograph is virtual Lady Zee now;
and that is how, to me, Zee will be in the future.
But beautiful as she is, the girl means
absolutely nothing to me, although the whole world, but
only in so far as she reminds me of
Lady Zee's breathtaking beauty.
Yes, Lady Zee's stunning sultry looks
will forever remain with me, since
'A thing of beauty is a joy forever.'

THE NIGHT OF THE NIGHTMARE

On that dark Saturday night
I was almost smothered to death
when Lady Zee unplugged the electrical
conduit connecting our two souls,
leaving me at the receiving end
without electrical power,
without the will to live.

At once I ran the gamut of depression,
devastation, migraines,
throbbing ear drums, a broken heart
and insomnia.
That's right, I slept not a wink
on the night of the nightmare.

When the emotional bombshell was dropped
on the night of the blackout,
I felt the ground beneath my feet giving way;
I felt my soul oozing out of me;
I felt a crucial part of me dying,
for my heart was about to snap,
and I was half in love with easeful death.

Again and again that dreadful night
I woke up to the bitter reality;
I woke up to face the terrible Truth;
I woke up to confront the Nightmare.
And there it was standing, huge like an Elephant:
the most beautiful and brilliant woman in my
life was about to slip through my fingers;
a crucial part of me was dying forever.
And like a child I wept like never before.
Yes, I was partially in love with painless death.

But thanks to Venus's timely intervention,
thanks to therapeutic sessions
of soul-to-soul telephone talks,
thanks to soul-searching sessions of
telephone conversations,
I have been rescued from death;
for we have electrically been reconnected
by the arrow from Cupid's bow.
At last I can now declare with relief:
Not Frankenstein, my name is Pigmalion.

LOOK UP IN THE SKY!

Look! Look!
Look up in the sky
and tell me what you see there.
Look at the moon.
Yes, the moon with two stars.
That is Lady Zee with her guardian stars,
the superluna in the company of the stars.

Look at the placement of the stars.
Look at how they stand.
Not equidistant from her,
one is nearer, the other farther.
One is weaker, the other stronger,
but both of whose breasts are
full of fire for her,
with their gaze gravitated towards her.

Not in known rivalry over her
each performs an assigned task:
the stronger is the roving star;
the weaker and supporter, the home-based star.
The latter is ready to surrender his role
as soon as the former regains his base.

The weaker star will gradually
fade out when the brighter one
takes sole control.
Nothing could be more natural.
That's right, the home-based star will behind the
mountain disappear as soon as the
itinerant powerful Ambikoh takes centre stage,
as soon as he returns to base at Sabga Heights
to resume his lunar dominance.

ATTEMPTING THE IMPOSSIBLE

It is easier for engineers
to construct from planet Earth to the moon
your super highway
than for me to wipe out from
my consciousness memories of Lady Zee.

A mega tower, built on a sounder
foundation, would sooner deliver
Earth's message at Heaven's Gate
than for me to deracinate from my mind
vestiges of Lady Zee's rule.

A glacial mountain melting at the slow
rate of a millimetre per century
would sooner melt away in a life-time
than for me to uproot from my psyche
the impact made by Lady Zee.

Que faire? It is better to cave in
than the impossible to attempt to do;
better to praise aloud than to try to wipe out her name;
better to glorify than to essay to nullify her fame;
better to sing abroad than to try to blot out her name.
Yes, Lady Zee deserves no less than this.

IF I WERE TO HATE MY LADY

Do I hate Lady Zee?
No; hate is hardly the right word
to describe my passion for Lady Zee;
hate is too strong but too weak a word
to convey my unique emotion
towards this exceptional woman.

To me Lady Zee is an object
intensely desirable;
she is very delicate and fragile.
Like an egg, she's to be handled with
care and love, and not scorn or hate.

A rare specie,
Lady Zee is charming, beautiful and brilliant.
But she adds to these sterling qualities
 admirable strength of character,
maturity and wisdom beyond her years.
Surely a woman like this should
inspire adulation, and not hate.

But, oh! If I were to hate my Lady!
Then world languages would have to be rewritten;
then humanity would have to reinvent itself
to look for a stronger word than hate
to convey the devastating power of my passion;
for I would not hate in short measure.
The impact of my hatred would be on a global scale.
If I were to hate my Lady,
then my hatred would be as big and deep
as my love for her;
then my anger, my emotional balloon,
would expand and fill the entire cosmos

as a boiled egg fills its shell.
And were this full balloon to explode,
then there would be no trace that life
ever existed on planet Earth;
then your atomic bomb would be a harmless toy
beside my exploded balloon.
And my hatred would have the effect of
a blood-dimmed tide flowing from Limbe,
passing through humid Mamfe,
to distant and cold Nkambe,
calcifying everything in its path
and then settling in Yaounde
to take on a national coloration
before assuming the form of
final, tidal waves of cosmic cataclysm.

TELEPATHY

Lady Zee
Sometimes, when in the middle of dialling
you, I have been stopped by your sudden call;
and occasionally, by your admission,
I have broken in on your thoughts
when you were thinking of me.
And so our cell phones have confirmed
our occasional, simultaneous thinking of each other.

We have often marvelled at the
coincidence of our thoughts, feelings and moods
and wondered why so.
And here I state the answer loud and clear:
Telepathy; it resides in telepathy.
That's right, the answer lies in the intriguing
communication of thoughts and feelings
between allied souls across distances.
Your brief message today was the occasion
for yet another telepathy,
the umpteenth telepathy!

Ever since your heart and my heart were pierced
by Cupid's arrow, our two souls have
interfused, becoming one entity.
But while our bodies are earthbound
our blended, purer soul has gravitated
towards a higher ethereal region,
the home of Royal Essence.

And like a stable satellite
our single soul, centre of our thoughts
and feelings, is lodged in an
inter-galactic orbit whence it emits

infrared romantic beams
that animate our earthbound bodies.
So our earthbound bodies – your body
and my body – and our quintessential soul
are in an isosceles triangular union.

Your body and my body both
constitute the base of the triangle
while its top is our superior soul.
And our soul, the Monarch of our bodies,
activates our two bodies through two
cosmic romantic rays.
These sentimental shafts of light,
equidistant from our galactic soul,
make up the two equal sides of the triangle,
and then connect with our two bodies.

Such being the case,
it is useless for our bodies to shun
each other; it is needless for us to
put up defences. What we fear
to yield has already been endorsed
by our purer soul, the inter-galactic tenant,
thanks to the triangular union
of our two bodies and our single soul.
They cannot be wrong, our earthbound bodies.
Therefore, our earthbound desires
cannot be termed dirt, for they
have been sanctioned by a higher
authority, our blended, superior single soul.

LADY ZEE'S REPLY:
THE SYMPHONY

Let me be the guitar
Slung across your firm chest
Held by your masterful arm
Close to your heart to love and cuddle
So gentle and muscular and strong.

Let me be the piano
That your confident fingers
Caress, tingle, lovingly touch
Your piano to play
With lingering loving music.

Let me be your lyrical drum
Your magical beat
Controlling the sweet rhythm
And the pulsating vibrations
Of our souls' romantic sensations.

EPITHALAMION
(ODE TO LADY ZEE)

1

Sisters Nine, offspring of Mnemosyne and Zeus!
Often when in search of inspiration
to praise others have I turned to you.
Olympian goddesses of inspiration,
Many a time have you come to my aid
in my hour of poetic parturition.
If you could help me to praise others
will you now abandon me when I
solicit the same succour for my own sake?
Hearken, therefore, Muses Nine, hearken to my appeal.
Come, therefore, members of Apollo's retinue.
Come to my rescue.
Come and help me to celebrate, in verse,
the day of my own glory.
Come and assist me to immortalise,
in poetry, the day I captured
the greatest woman on earth.

2

Go! Messengers, go!
Go and tell the world here and abroad
that the news is out that will transform me;
that the word has been pronounced that will
make me a superman, for Lady Zee
has given her consent that before the day
runs its full course, we shall both be
candidates at Hymen's holy shrine.
Proclaim the good tidings with trumpet
and the calling drum.
Declare the good news over hills and valleys

that the whole world may hear:
Go! Dudum messengers, go!
Drum! Dudum drummers, drum!
Send the message through the calling drum,
from one Dudum drum to another
that Dudum valleys may resound with thunderous echoes.

3

You, nymphs of Dudum woods,
and you, mermaids of Dudum falls and rivers,
You, delicate sylphs of Dudum skies,
and you, darling fairies of Dudum forests,
arise and fly to Lady Zee's abode.
Go and whisper into the ears of my Love.
Tell her that the day is here that I will
make her what she least dreamed of: the greatest woman
in the whole world.
Yes, go and inform her before the sun
appears in the east to chase away
the darkness of the night from Dudum land.
Go! Dudum mermaids, go!
Drum! Dudum drummers, drum!
Send the message through the calling drum,
from one Dudum drum to another
that Dudum valleys may resound with thunderous echoes.

4

Make the way clear for Lady Zee.
Open up the path for her to pass through.
Yes, the Queen of the Universe is up
and ready to make straight for the place
of ceremony.
All seamstresses and all attendants,
Get ready to deck your Mistress in her

freshest and finest attire.
Select from the best wardrobe what will
make this paragon of beauty
more unparalleled in world beauty.
But first watch what you yourselves are
wearing, lest you offend her delicate taste.
Go! Attendants, go!
Drum! Dudum drummers, drum!
Send the message through the calling drum,
from one Dudum drum to another
that the Dudum valleys may resound with thunderous echoes.

5

You, choral groups of Dudum country church.
Come out with all your best melodies.
Select from your repertoire the best rally songs
most of which have thrilled many a soul,
and for which you have won many a trophy
on many a rally ground in all of Dudum land.
Yes, you Madrigal, bring out your best.
And you, CYF, let your fingers drum
on the skin-drum to produce those soul-
elevating sounds that have pulled many
to our church.
And you Bethel, where are you?
Bethel Choir, bring out your best songs
that have lifted many souls to Heaven's gate.
Go! Bethel Choir, go!
Drum! Dudum drummers, drum!
Send the message through the calling drum,
from one Dudum drum to another
that Dudum valleys may resound with thunderous echoes.

6

The bridal party is on its way to
the ceremonial ground.
Lady Zee is in their midst to the festive scene.
But Lady Zee will not budge an inch until
cash from the groom's coffers flows easily.
Lady Zee will not walk fast until the
groom has proven his worth in terms of wealth.
So, let the bride be showered with wealth.
Let my wealth around Lady Zee flow
so that she can begin to walk faster.
Now, around the bride brand new bills are falling.
Around my Love countless coins are pouring down.
And jubilant are all the relatives
picking up the sprinkled cash around Lady Zee.
Now, messengers, trumpet the word abroad
that the bride is moving faster at last!
Go! Dudum messengers, go!
Drum! Dudum drummers, drum!
Send the message through the calling drum,
from one Dudum drum to another
that the Dudum valleys may resound with thunderous
echoes.

7

In the country church they are now gathered.
Christians young and old are all seated,
clad in their multicoloured expensive attire.
Music from choral groups rings from corner
to corner, as with throaty voices and
harmonious instruments they make a joyful
noise unto Heaven.
The church vibrates with heavenly music
as the faithful await the bridal party.

In four rows they await, the faithful await;
in four rows of 20 pews they joyfully
await the arrival of the celebrities,
while, in turn, choirs from four key corners
of the church thrill all and sundry with
soul-lifting songs that the outside world
should be informed of:
Go! Dudum messengers, go!
Drum! Dudum drummers, drum!
Send the message through the calling drum,
from one Dudum drum to another
that Dudum valleys may resound with thunderous echoes.

8

The couple is at the entrance to the church.
The festooned archway is loaded with fresh flowers.
And thick in the air is the sweet fragrance
of a profusion of country flowers.
Ask not where the flower girls are.
They are there, six in number, in their
beautiful dresses and with their bouquets of flowers.
Ask not where the pageboys are.
They too are there, six in number, in their
trim attire, and ready to put things in order.
The bridesmaids, ask not about the bridesmaids,
for they too are there.
Well- selected beauties in their own right,
the bridesmaids are there, and any could
easily pass for the bride herself.
As for the groomsmen they too are there.
In their well-cut black suits they are
Dudum's models of strength and handsomeness.
So Dudum drummers should inform the out-
side world of this. Go! Dudum drummers, go!
Drum! Dudum drummers, drum!

Send the message through the calling drum,
from one Dudum drum to another
that Dudum valleys may resound with thunderous echoes.

9

And the couple, now is their turn;
the couple cannot be left out here.
First the groom, the groom must be mentioned first.
And many are those who have said to have
captured such an earthly glory as Lady
Zee, the groom must have been a superstar
himself; so by general consent the groom
is said to be a notch or two above
the best of the groomsmen, and with that
we need say no more about him.
And now to the bride, we must now turn to the bride.
We must now turn to the trophy of the day.
We must now look at Lady Zee the bride.
With a soft silky skin of chocolate
complexion Lady Zee possesses
stunning sultry looks that would turn
many a beauty green with envy.
In her stainless white and flowing wedding gown
with a delicate but transparent veil
thrown over her head and shoulders, Lady
Zee is the epitomy of female beauty,
now Queen of Dudum Clan.
We therefore have only one appeal to make:
Go! Dudum messengers, go!
Drum! Dudum drummers, drum!
Send the message through the calling drum,
from one Dudum drum to another
that the Dudum valleys may resound with thunderous echoes.

10

The procession is moving into the church;
the bride and the groom are now moving in.
Let the faithful stand up to receive them.
Led by the flower girls and the pageboys,
the bridal party is moving into
the church following a slow, solemn song by
the Madrigal Choir and a piano.
The bridal pilot squirts from a device
coloured, perfumed flakes above the heads
of those processing.
But above and over the heads of the
couple, coloured flakes come down in great profusion.
But by and by the couple soon gain the altar
where to tie the knot the priest is waiting,
information worth trumpeting abroad,
even as far as Sabga Heights,
with the help of the calling drum:
Go, Dudum messengers, go!
Drum! Dudum drummers, drum!
Send the message through the calling drum,
from one Dudum drum to another
that Dudum valleys may resound with thunderous echoes.

11

And now is the time for the final act,
now the time for the final word,
the crescendo of all our little loves,
the raison d'etre of the courtship poems.
And now my beautiful and brilliant Lady Zee,
by the power of all the amoretti;
by the strength of magic telepathy;
by the force of fantastic SS;
in the name of the moon and the two stars;

in the name of your own word «Peut-etre»;
in the name of sweet 'Symphony'
I implore you to put your hand in mine
before the priest and the congregation
to affirm that we are husband and wife.
Ah! Yes, she does, and the act is done.
«Both of you are husband and wife, today»,
the priest confirms by raising high our hands.
And thunderous is the standing ovation
that deserves to be extended abroad
through the sound of the calling drum:
Go! Dudum drummers, go!
Drum! Dudum drummers, drum!
Send the message through the calling drum
from one Dudum drum to another
that Dudum valleys may resound with thunderous echoes.

12

Now that in church the rite is over,
outside the church feasting should begin.
Let victuals of all sorts be on display.
Let viands of all kinds satisfy all tastes.
Let beers of all brands fill the tables
and wines from all climes indulge every tongue.
The sun is shining in our hearts
as it is shining on Dudum Land.
Our joy is full and complete
and our cup is running over.
Therefore, let the wine flow abundantly,
not in calabashes nor in jugs
but in drums and in barrels.
Let it flow like water from the tap.
But no Bacchanalian celebration
is tolerated here; nor are Dionysian
orgies permitted here.

In this Christian wedding moderation
is the order of the day.
Let celebrants drink to their fill.
Let revellers drink and roar aloud
so that drummers can take over the song:
Go! Dudum drummers, go!
Drum! Dudum drummers drum!
Send the message through the calling drum,
from one Dudum drum to another
that Dudum valleys may resound with thunderous echoes.

13

All day long are heard joyous sounds of
celebration from all corners of the clan;
all day long are heard happy songs of
festivities from all parts of Dudum Clan.
From one end of Dudum Clan to another,
are fired staccato gunshots of revelry.
But as evening draws near,
as the sun draws nearer and nearer to the west,
so too begins to diminish the intensity of festivity;
so to begins to decline the ardour of jubilee;
so too begins to dwindle the number of wedding guests;
so too begins to die down the clamour of carousal.
And as darkness envelopes Dudum Clan,
all sounds are smothered, and nothing is heard,
for from the festive scene have all guests disappeared.
So there is no Dudum drum to be drummed,
and no message to be sent from one
Dudum drum to another.
Therefore, there will be no resounding
echoes to be heard from Dudum valleys.

14

Now the festivities are over.
Tonight we are the world reduced to our bedroom.
Beyond these four walls nothing else matters.
And no one can reproach us for whatever
we do here and now.
Our inter-galactic single soul
had earlier confirmed our union.
Before man and God the Priest ratified
it in church this morning.
What our earthbound bodies feel cannot be wrong.
Therefore, our earthbound desires
cannot be termed dirt.
So, come into our conjugal bed, baby.
Come, without delay, come my dear Zee.
Come into our sanctified marital bed.
Leave aside your usual coyness;
leave it aside.
Put away your accustomed shyness;
put it away.
Coyness has no place in our case tonight.
Whatever we do here
ends within the four walls of our bedroom.
There is no Dudum drum to be drummed
and no message to be sent from one
Dudum drum to another.
Therefore, there will be no resounding
echoes to be heard from the Dudum valleys.

15

Lady Zee is now in my arms, my glory.
Like the moon and her galaxy of stars,
may we be blessed with numerous progeny
to be brought up in the fear of the Lord.
From now till dawn let nothing disturb us.
And for this we call on you, magic Orpheus.
Come to us, Apollo's protégé.
Come and, by our window, install yourself,
at least for our sake only tonight.
Through the powers and sweetness of your music you
charmed boulders to encircle you;
you charmed trees to follow you;
you charmed your way into perilous
Hades in quest of your late Eurydice.
By the same token, magic Orpheus,
employ your magical, lyrical powers
to charm away demons from our door;
to charm away nightmares from our room;
to charm away evil men from our yard
that we may have a peaceful sleep tonight.
But, above all, charm us into sweet dreams.
And that as we dream sweet dreams,
there will be no Dudum drum to be drummed
and no message to be sent from one Dudum
drum to another.
Therefore, there will be no resounding
echoes to be heard from Dudum valleys.

16

A nuptial song composed in the place of
wedding presents that could never match the beauty of
the bard's bride. It is hoped that
the public will take it for what it is:
a momentary whim in the manner of
the superior ancient poetic masters.

Titles by *Langaa* RPCIG

Francis B. Nyamnjoh
Stories from Abakwa
Mind Searching
The Disillusioned African
The Convert
Souls Forgotten
Married But Available
Intimate Strangers

Dibussi Tande
No Turning Back. Poems of Freedom 1990-1993
Scribbles from the Den: Essays on Politics and Collective
Memory in Cameroon

Kangsen Feka Wakai
Fragmented Melodies

Ntemfac Ofege
Namondo. Child of the Water Spirits
Hot Water for the Famous Seven

Emmanuel Fru Doh
Not Yet Damascus
The Fire Within
Africa's Political Wastelands: The Bastardization of
Cameroon
Oriki'badan
Wading the Tide
Stereotyping Africa: Surprising Answers to Surprising
Questions

Thomas Jing
Tale of an African Woman

Peter Wuteh Vakunta
Grassfields Stories from Cameroon
Green Rape: Poetry for the Environment
Majunga Tok: Poems in Pidgin English
Cry, My Beloved Africa
No Love Lost
Straddling The Mungo: A Book of Poems in English
& French

Ba'bila Mutia
Coils of Mortal Flesh

Kehbuma Langmia
Titabet and the Takumbeng
An Evil Meal of Evil
The Earth Mother

Victor Elame Musinga
The Barn
The Tragedy of Mr. No Balance

Ngessimo Mathe Mutaka
Building Capacity: Using TEFL and African Languages as
Development-oriented Literacy Tools

Milton Krieger
Cameroon's Social Democratic Front: Its History and
Prospects as an Opposition Political Party, 1990-2011

Sammy Oke Akombi
The Raped Amulet
The Woman Who Ate Python
Beware the Drives: Book of Verse
The Wages of Corruption

Susan Nkwentie Nde
Precipice
Second Engagement

Francis B. Nyamnjoh & Richard Fonteh Akum
The Cameroon GCE Crisis: A Test of Anglophone
Solidarity

Joyce Ashuntantang & Dibussi Tande
Their Champagne Party Will End! Poems in Honor of
Bate Besong

Emmanuel Achu
Disturbing the Peace

Rosemary Ekosso
The House of Falling Women

Peterkins Manyong
God the Politician

George Ngwane
The Power in the Writer: Collected Essays on Culture,
Democracy & Development in Africa

John Percival
The 1961 Cameroon Plebiscite: Choice or Betrayal

Albert Azeyeh
Réussite scolaire, faillite sociale : généalogie mentale de
la crise de l'Afrique noire francophone

Aloysius Ajab Amin & Jean-Luc Dubois
Croissance et développement au Cameroun :
d'une croissance équilibrée à un développement équitable

Carlson Anyangwe
Imperialistic Politics in Cameroun:
Resistance & the Inception of the Restoration of the
Statehood of Southern Cameroons
Betrayal of Too Trusting a People: The UN, the UK and
the Trust Territory of the Southen Cameroons

Bill F. Ndi
K'Cracy, Trees in the Storm and Other Poems
Map: Musings On Ars Poetica
Thomas Lurting: The Fighting Sailor Turn'd Peaceable /
Le marin combattant devenu paisible
Soleil et ombre

**Kathryn Toure, Therese Mungah
Shalo Tchombe & Thierry Karsenti**
ICT and Changing Mindsets in Education

Charles Alobwed'Epie
The Day God Blinked
The Bad Samaritan
The Lady with the Sting

G. D. Nyamndi
Babi Yar Symphony
Whether losing, Whether winning
Tussles: Collected Plays
Dogs in the Sun

Samuel Ebelle Kingue
Si Dieu était tout un chacun de nous ?

Ignasio Malizani Jimu
Urban Appropriation and Transformation: bicycle, taxi
and handcart operators in Mzuzu, Malawi

Justice Nyo' Wakai
Under the Broken Scale of Justice: The Law and My
Times

John Eyong Mengot
A Pact of Ages

Ignasio Malizani Jimu
Urban Appropriation and Transformation: Bicycle Taxi
and Handcart Operators

Joyce B. Ashuntantang
Landscaping and Coloniality: The Dissemination of
Cameroon Anglophone Literature
I Cry When It's Cold

Jude Fokwang
Mediating Legitimacy: Chieftaincy and Democratisation in
Two African Chiefdoms